Present with Impact

Presentation skill guide book

Bhagyashree Kindre

Table to Content.

Introduction

In the realm of professional communication, the ability to deliver impactful presentations is an indispensable skill. Whether you are a seasoned executive, an aspiring entrepreneur, or a student preparing for a class presentation, mastering the art of presenting with impact can elevate your message and leave a lasting impression on your audience.

The Power of Effective Presentations

The introductory chapter sets the stage by highlighting the significance of effective presentations in various aspects of life. Presentations are not mere displays of information; they are opportunities to connect, persuade, and inspire. In today's fast-paced world, where attention spans are fleeting, the need to convey messages compellingly has never been more critical.

Presentations serve as a gateway to effective communication, allowing ideas to transcend the boundaries of words and resonate with the audience on a deeper level. Whether you're pitching a business proposal, delivering a motivational speech, or simply sharing insights with colleagues, the impact of your presentation hinges on your ability to engage, inform, and leave a lasting impression.

Understanding the Audience

This chapter delves into the foundational element of impactful presentations – understanding the audience. To truly connect with your listeners, it is crucial to grasp their needs, expectations, and perspectives. By tailoring your message to align with the interests of your audience, you create a more profound connection and increase the likelihood of your message being received positively.

The chapter explores strategies for audience analysis, emphasizing the importance of adapting your communication style to resonate with diverse groups. Whether addressing a boardroom full of professionals or presenting to a classroom of students, the ability to tailor your content to suit your audience's preferences is a skill that can set you apart as a communicator.

Crafting a Compelling Message

The journey to impactful presentations continues with a focus on crafting a compelling message. An effective presentation is built upon a solid foundation – a clear and concise core message. This section explores the art of distilling complex ideas into key points, ensuring that your audience grasps and retains the essence of your presentation.

Readers are guided through the process of structuring their presentations for optimal clarity. Techniques for organizing content in a logical and engaging manner are discussed, empowering presenters to captivate their audience from the opening statement to the final conclusion.

Powerful Openings

As the saying goes, "You never get a second chance to make a first impression." This chapter underscores the importance of powerful openings in presentations. Readers learn various techniques to grab their audience's attention right from the start, setting a positive and engaging tone for the rest of the presentation.

From compelling anecdotes to thought-provoking questions, the chapter explores creative ways to draw listeners into the presentation, ensuring that they remain attentive and receptive throughout. The power of a strong opening is unraveled, emphasizing its role in creating a memorable and impactful presentation experience.

In conclusion, Chapter 1 establishes the foundation for the reader's journey into the world of impactful presentations. By emphasizing the importance of effective communication, understanding the audience, crafting a compelling message, and delivering powerful openings, the stage is set for a comprehensive exploration of presentation skills in the subsequent chapters. As readers delve deeper into the art and science of presentations, they are equipped with the knowledge and tools to elevate their communication prowess and leave a lasting impact on their audiences.

Understanding Your Audience

In the intricate dance of effective presentations, the choreography extends beyond the speaker to encompass the audience. Chapter 2 delves into the nuanced art of understanding your audience an essential element in the alchemy of impactful communication.

The Audience-Centric Approach

The chapter unfolds with a fundamental principle: an audience-centric approach is the linchpin of successful presentations. Presenters are guided through the process of empathizing with their audience, stepping into their shoes to comprehend their perspectives, expectations, and needs. This empathetic lens forms the bedrock upon which impactful presentations are built.

By cultivating a deep understanding of the audience, presenters can tailor their content to resonate with the collective consciousness of their listeners. Whether addressing a group of industry experts hungry for technical details or a general audience seeking relatable anecdotes, the ability to align the presentation with audience expectations lays the groundwork for connection and engagement.

Strategies for Audience Analysis

The chapter introduces practical strategies for conducting audience analysis, ensuring that presenters embark on their communication journey armed with insights. From demographic considerations to cultural nuances, readers are equipped with a toolkit to decipher the unique composition of their audience. Understanding the professional background, interests, and knowledge level of the audience becomes pivotal in crafting content that is not only informative but also relevant and accessible.

The exploration of audience personas adds a human touch to the process, enabling presenters to create a mental image of their target audience. By segmenting the audience into distinct personas, each with its unique characteristics, presenters can tailor their message to resonate with diverse segments, fostering a sense of inclusivity and connection.

Adapting Communication Styles

As the chapter unfolds, attention shifts to the adaptive nature of effective communication. Presenters are encouraged to flex their communication styles to match the preferences of their audience. Whether it's adopting a more formal tone for a corporate setting or infusing humor and anecdotes for a more casual audience, the ability to adapt enhances the presenter's relatability.

Understanding cultural nuances also plays a pivotal role in adapting communication styles. Respectful consideration of cultural differences ensures that the presentation is not only inclusive but also avoids inadvertently causing offense. The chapter navigates the delicate balance between universal communication principles and the need for cultural sensitivity.

Tailoring Content for Maximum Relevance

The final sections of Chapter 2 guide presenters in the art of tailoring content for maximum relevance. Through the strategic alignment of the presentation's key messages with the identified needs and expectations of the audience, presenters can create a seamless connection.

Readers are encouraged to conduct pre-presentation surveys or engage in pre-event discussions to gather audience insights. This proactive approach allows presenters to fine-tune their content, ensuring that it not only addresses the audience's current concerns but also anticipates potential questions or points of interest.

In essence, Chapter 2 serves as a compass, guiding presenters through the intricate terrain of audience dynamics. By mastering the art of understanding their audience, presenters lay the groundwork for impactful communication that transcends the confines of information delivery. As the chapter unfolds, readers are equipped with the tools to navigate the intricacies of diverse audiences, fostering connection and engagement in their presentation endeavours.

Crafting a Compelling Message

In the symphony of impactful presentations, Chapter 3 emerges as the maestro, orchestrating the elements that transform information into inspiration. This chapter delves into the art and science of crafting a compelling message—a crucial pillar in the architecture of presentations that resonate and endure in the minds of the audience.

The Essence of a Core Message

At the heart of every impactful presentation lies a core message a concise and powerful statement encapsulating the essence of the speaker's purpose. Chapter 3 begins by unravelling the significance of distilling complex ideas into a clear and memorable core message. Readers are guided through the process of identifying the primary takeaway, ensuring that the audience leaves with a distinct understanding of the key message.

The chapter emphasizes the transformative power of simplicity, encouraging presenters to resist the allure of information overload. By focusing on a singular, well-articulated message, presenters can cut through the noise and deliver a presentation that is not only memorable but also actionable.

Structuring for Impactful Delivery

With the core message as the North Star, the chapter navigates the terrain of presentation structure. Presenters are introduced to techniques that enhance clarity and engagement, such as the classic three-act structure or variations like problem-solution narratives. The art of sequencing ideas to create a logical flow becomes paramount, ensuring that the audience is taken on a journey of understanding, revelation, and resolution.

Strategic placement of key points, supported by compelling evidence or anecdotes, is explored as a means to reinforce the core message. The chapter unveils the power of a well-structured presentation in capturing and maintaining audience attention, a fundamental aspect of delivering impact.

Visual Storytelling and Persuasion

The visual component of presentations is illuminated in this chapter, underscoring the adage that a picture is worth a thousand words. Visual storytelling emerges as a powerful tool for reinforcing the core message, with techniques such as the use of compelling images, infographics, and minimalistic slides discussed in detail.

Readers are guided through the art of persuasion, exploring how visual elements can complement verbal communication to create a more persuasive narrative. The strategic use of visuals not only enhances audience understanding but also evokes emotional responses, fostering a deeper connection between the presenter and the audience.

Anticipating and Addressing Questions

The chapter concludes by addressing a critical aspect of crafting a compelling message—anticipating and addressing audience questions. Presenters are encouraged to adopt a proactive stance by incorporating potential queries into the presentation structure. By doing so, presenters not only demonstrate thorough knowledge but also convey a genuine willingness to engage with the audience.

The importance of fostering an interactive environment is highlighted, where questions are welcomed rather than feared. Techniques for handling spontaneous questions with grace and composure are explored, empowering presenters to navigate the Q&A session with confidence.

In summary, Chapter 3 serves as a beacon for presenters navigating the intricate process of crafting a compelling message. By understanding the significance of a core message, mastering presentation structure, embracing visual storytelling, and proactively addressing audience questions, presenters equip themselves with the tools to captivate and resonate with their audience. As the chapter unfolds, the reader is invited to embark on a journey of strategic communication, where every word and image contributes to the creation of a presentation that lingers in the minds of the audience long after the last slide.

Powerful Openings

As the curtains rise on Chapter 4, the spotlight is cast on a pivotal element in the presentation performance—the powerful opening. In the theatre of impactful communication, the first moments on stage hold the potential to captivate, intrigue, and set the tone for an unforgettable experience. This chapter explores the art and strategies behind creating powerful openings that grab the audience's attention from the outset.

The Art of Captivation

The chapter unfolds by emphasizing the transformative impact of a compelling introduction. Presenters are guided to view the opening moments as a precious window of opportunity—a chance to establish rapport, pique curiosity, and lay the groundwork for an engaging narrative.

Readers are encouraged to consider the emotional journey they wish to take their audience on and to craft openings that resonate with the overarching theme of the presentation. Whether through a thought-provoking question, a captivating story, or a surprising statistic, the art of captivation becomes the guiding principle.

Understanding Audience Psychology

A significant portion of Chapter 4 is dedicated to unravelling the psychology of audiences during the opening moments of a presentation. Presenters are invited to consider the audience's natural inclination to form initial impressions rapidly. Strategies to leverage this psychological phenomenon are explored, emphasizing the importance of authenticity and relevance in creating a strong first impression.

The chapter delves into the power of relatability, urging presenters to connect with their audience on a human level. By understanding and acknowledging the audience's concerns or interests right from the start, presenters can forge a stronger bond and evoke a sense of shared experience.

Techniques for Powerful Openings

The practical toolkit for crafting powerful openings is unveiled in this chapter, offering presenters a range of techniques to suit various presentation contexts. From the impactful use of humour to the artful incorporation of anecdotes, presenters are empowered to choose methods that align with their style and the nature of their presentation.

The chapter explores the strategic use of rhetorical questions, inviting the audience to actively participate in the thought process. This engagement not only captures attention but also sets the stage for a more interactive and dynamic presentation.

Setting the Tone for the Presentation

Beyond mere captivation, Chapter 4 underscores the role of powerful openings in setting the tone for the entire presentation. Presenters are encouraged to consider the emotional atmosphere they wish to cultivate and to align the opening with the overarching mood of the presentation.

For presentations that aim to inspire, motivate, or instigate action, the chapter introduces techniques to infuse openings with a sense of purpose and urgency. The objective is to evoke an emotional response that resonates throughout the entirety of the presentation, leaving a lasting impact on the audience.

Practice and Refinement

The chapter concludes with an essential reminder—the importance of practice and refinement in perfecting the art of powerful openings. Presenters are guided to rehearse their introductions with a focus on timing, delivery, and audience response. By honing this critical element, presenters can instil confidence in their ability to capture attention and make a compelling first impression.

In essence, Chapter 4 serves as a masterclass in the art of powerful openings. By appreciating the transformative impact of the initial moments, understanding audience psychology, exploring a diverse range of techniques, and setting the tone for the presentation, presenters are equipped to elevate their communication prowess. As the curtain falls on this chapter, readers are invited to embark on a journey where every presentation begins with a captivating overture, ensuring that the audience is not merely present but fully engaged from the very first note.

Effective Visuals in Presentations

As the narrative unfolds in Chapter 5, the spotlight shifts to the visual dimension of impactful presentations. Visuals serve as the silent choreographers, complementing the spoken word and breathing life into the message. This chapter delves into the principles and strategies of leveraging effective visuals to enhance understanding, engagement, and retention.

The Visual Advantage

The chapter begins by underscoring the inherent advantages of incorporating visuals into presentations. In a world where attention is a precious currency, visuals act as attention magnets, guiding the audience's focus and reinforcing key messages. Readers are prompted to recognize the cognitive benefits of visual aids, acknowledging that well-designed visuals can transcend language barriers and resonate with diverse learning styles.

Understanding the symbiotic relationship between visuals and spoken content becomes crucial. Whether through slides, infographics, or multimedia elements, visuals have the power to amplify the impact of a presentation and leave a lasting impression.

Creating Visually Appealing Slides

A significant portion of Chapter 5 is devoted to the art of crafting visually appealing slides. Presenters are guided through the principles of simplicity, clarity, and coherence in slide design. The strategic use of colours, fonts, and layouts is explored, ensuring that the visual elements harmonize with the overall theme of the presentation.

Readers are encouraged to embrace the mantra of less is more, resisting the temptation to overcrowd slides with excessive text or complex graphics. By distilling information into digestible visual nuggets, presenters can foster a connection with the audience and enhance the overall visual appeal.

Visual Storytelling Techniques

The narrative unfolds into the realm of visual storytelling, where the synergy of images and narrative weaves a compelling tapestry. This chapter introduces readers to techniques such as the use of metaphors, analogies, and symbolism in visual storytelling. By infusing visuals with narrative elements, presenters can transform data into relatable stories that resonate with the audience on an emotional level.

Strategies for creating a visual narrative arc, akin to the traditional three-act structure, are explored. This approach not only guides the audience through a cohesive visual journey but also fosters a sense of anticipation and resolution.

Incorporating Graphics and Images

Chapter 5 places a spotlight on the strategic use of graphics and images to convey complex information. Infographics emerge as powerful tools for distilling intricate data into visually digestible formats. The chapter offers guidance on choosing the right type of graphics to complement specific types of information, ensuring that visuals enhance rather than distract from the core message.

Presenters are encouraged to select images that evoke emotion and reinforce the narrative. The impact of carefully chosen visuals in evoking a desired emotional response is discussed, highlighting their ability to enhance audience connection and engagement.

Balancing Visuals with Verbal Communication

An essential aspect of this chapter is the exploration of balance—finding the sweet spot where visuals and verbal communication harmonize. Presenters are guided to use visuals as supplements rather than replacements for spoken words. The chapter emphasizes the importance of maintaining a verbal narrative that complements and elaborates on the visual content, creating a seamless and immersive presentation experience.

Technology and Interactivity

The chapter concludes with a forward gaze into the evolving landscape of presentation technology and interactivity. Presenters are prompted to consider how emerging tools, such as interactive presentations or virtual reality, can elevate the visual dimension of their presentations. While acknowledging the potential of technology, the chapter emphasizes that effective visuals ultimately hinge on thoughtful design and relevance to the audience.

In summary, Chapter 5 serves as a beacon for presenters navigating the visual landscape of presentations. By understanding the advantages of visuals, mastering the art of slide design, embracing visual storytelling techniques, incorporating graphics and images, and balancing visuals with verbal communication, presenters are equipped to create presentations that captivate, resonate, and leave a lasting visual imprint on their audience. As the curtains fall on this chapter, readers are invited to embark on a visual journey where every slide contributes to the symphony of impactful communication.

Body Language and Non-Verbal Communication

As the narrative unfolds in Chapter 6, the focus pivots to the silent language that speaks volumes the realm of body language and non-verbal communication. Within the tapestry of impactful presentations, these unspoken cues form a dynamic and influential layer, shaping the audience's perception and interpretation. This chapter unravels the intricacies of body language, offering insights into its power, nuances, and strategic application.

The Silent Communicator: Body Language

The chapter commences by highlighting the profound impact of body language as a silent communicator. Presenters are urged to recognize that, beyond the spoken word, their physical demeanour, facial expressions, and gestures convey a rich tapestry of meaning to the audience. The significance of authenticity in body language is underscored, emphasizing the alignment between verbal and non-verbal cues for a cohesive and trustworthy presentation.

Understanding the nuances of body language enables presenters to harness its potential as a tool for connection, engagement, and influence. Readers are guided through the exploration of various components, from eye contact to posture, that collectively contribute to the silent dialogue between the presenter and the audience.

Facial Expressions: The Canvas of Emotion

A significant portion of the chapter is dedicated to the canvas of emotion—facial expressions. Presenters are encouraged to view their facial expressions as a reflection of the emotional landscape of their presentation. Techniques for conveying sincerity, enthusiasm, and empathy through facial expressions are explored, allowing presenters to create an emotional connection with their audience.

The chapter delves into the role of micro expressions subtle, fleeting facial expressions that convey authentic emotions. Presenters are prompted to heighten their awareness of these micro signals, as they can provide valuable insights into the presenter's genuine feelings and intentions.

Gestures and Posture: Choreographing the Presentation

The narrative unfolds into the realm of gestures and posture, where the presenter becomes a choreographer, using movement to accentuate key points and convey meaning. The chapter explores the art of purposeful gestures, highlighting their role in emphasizing concepts, maintaining audience engagement, and enhancing overall expressiveness.

Presenters are guided through the nuances of posture, from the confident stance that exudes authority to the open and approachable posture that fosters connection. The strategic use of movement and positioning within the presentation space is also discussed, underscoring the impact of physical dynamics on audience perception.

Eye Contact: The Bridge to Connection

Chapter 6 places a special emphasis on the significance of eye contact as the bridge to connection. The eyes are hailed as powerful conveyors of sincerity, confidence, and engagement. Presenters are encouraged to cultivate a balance, establishing eye contact with different segments of the audience to foster inclusivity and connection.

The chapter explores the psychology of eye contact, unveiling its role in building trust and rapport. Techniques for maintaining eye contact without veering into discomfort or intimidation are shared, empowering presenters to wield this silent communicator with finesse.

Adaptability and Cultural Sensitivity

As the chapter unfolds, the spotlight extends to the principles of adaptability and cultural sensitivity in non-verbal communication. Presenters are prompted to recognize that cultural norms and individual preferences can influence the interpretation of body language. Strategies for adapting one's non-verbal communication style to diverse audiences are explored, ensuring that the silent language resonates across cultural boundaries.

Conclusion: The Dance of Non-Verbal Communication

In conclusion, Chapter 6 encapsulates the intricate dance of body language and non-verbal communication within the context of impactful presentations. By unravelling the power of facial expressions, gestures, posture, and eye contact, and emphasizing adaptability to diverse audiences, presenters are equipped to choreograph a silent symphony that enhances their spoken message. As the chapter concludes, readers are invited to embrace the art of non-verbal communication, recognizing its ability to elevate presentations into compelling and authentic experiences.

Engaging Delivery Techniques

As the narrative unfolds in Chapter 7, the spotlight turns to the dynamic and transformative art of delivery—the bridge between content creation and audience connection. In the symphony of impactful presentations, this chapter explores the techniques that transform information into a compelling, engaging, and memorable experience for the audience.

The Essence of Engaging Delivery

The chapter commences by delving into the essence of engaging delivery, emphasizing that it extends beyond the words spoken. Engaging delivery encapsulates the entire presentation experience, encompassing tone, pacing, vocal variety, and the ability to connect with the audience on an emotional level. Readers are prompted to view the delivery as a performance an opportunity to captivate and leave a lasting impression.

Understanding the nuances of engaging delivery empowers presenters to transcend mere information-sharing and immerse their audience in an interactive and dynamic experience. The chapter guides readers through the exploration of various techniques that contribute to a delivery that resonates.

Tone and Vocal Variety: The Palette of Expression

A significant portion of the chapter is devoted to the expressive qualities of tone and vocal variety. Presenters are encouraged to recognize their voice as a versatile instrument, capable of conveying a spectrum of emotions and nuances. Techniques for modulating tone, pitch, and pace are explored, allowing presenters to infuse vitality and colour into their spoken words.

The chapter highlights the power of intentional pauses, where silence becomes a tool for emphasis, reflection, and audience engagement. By mastering the art of vocal variety, presenters can transform their delivery into a captivating journey that holds the audience's attention and fosters a deeper connection.

Dynamic Presentation Styles

The narrative unfolds into the realm of dynamic presentation styles, acknowledging that no two presenters are alike, and each possesses a unique style. Presenters are encouraged to embrace their authentic style while incorporating elements that enhance engagement. Whether it's injecting humour, storytelling, or interactive elements, the chapter explores diverse approaches to captivate and maintain audience interest.

The importance of adapting presentation styles to suit the nature of the content and the preferences of the audience is underscored. By aligning the presentation style with the message and the audience's expectations, presenters can create a seamless and resonant experience.

Interactive Techniques: Audience Participation

Chapter 7 places a spotlight on the interactive dimension of engaging delivery audience participation. Presenters are guided through techniques that invite the audience to actively participate in the presentation, transforming it from a passive experience into a shared journey.

Strategies for incorporating Q&A sessions, polls, discussions, and interactive exercises are explored. By fostering a sense of participation, presenters not only enhance engagement but also create a collaborative atmosphere where the audience becomes an integral part of the presentation.

Adapting to the Audience's Energy

The chapter unfolds into the principle of energy adaptation, urging presenters to attune themselves to the energy of the audience. Techniques for calibrating one's delivery to match the audience's mood, responsiveness, and preferences are shared. The ability to read the room and make real-time adjustments contributes to a presentation that feels responsive, dynamic, and attuned to the audience's needs.

Effective Use of Visual Aids

Visual aids, though discussed in Chapter 5, make a reappearance in Chapter 7 from a delivery perspective. Presenters are guided on the effective integration of visuals into the presentation, using them as supplementary tools to reinforce key points, rather than distractions. Techniques for seamlessly transitioning between spoken words and visual elements are explored, ensuring that the visual aids enhance, rather than overshadow, the delivery.

Conclusion: The Art and Impact of Delivery

In conclusion, Chapter 7 encapsulates the art and impact of engaging delivery in the presentation journey. By understanding the essence of engaging delivery, mastering tone and vocal variety, exploring dynamic presentation styles, incorporating interactive techniques, and adapting to the audience's energy, presenters are equipped to transform their presentations into compelling and memorable experiences. As the chapter concludes, readers are invited to embrace the role of the presenter as a performer, recognizing the transformative power of engaging delivery in creating presentations that resonate and endure in the minds of the audience.

Handling Questions and Feedback

As the narrative unfolds in Chapter 8, the focus turns to the interactive and dynamic phase of presentations—handling questions and feedback. This chapter navigates the intricacies of engaging with the audience's inquiries and opinions, transforming what might be perceived as a challenge into an opportunity for connection, clarification, and enhancement of the overall presentation experience.

The Importance of Interaction

The chapter begins by underscoring the crucial role of interaction in presentations. Q&A sessions and feedback segments represent a unique juncture where the audience actively engages with the presenter, contributing to a dynamic and collaborative environment. Readers are prompted to view questions and feedback not as obstacles but as valuable components that enrich the presentation dialogue.

Recognizing that audience participation fosters a more inclusive and interactive presentation, the chapter lays the foundation for effective strategies to handle questions and feedback with finesse.

Creating an Inclusive Q&A Atmosphere

Presenters are guided through the art of creating an inclusive atmosphere during Q&A sessions. Techniques for encouraging audience participation, whether through open invitations, designated question breaks, or interactive polls, are explored. By fostering an environment where questions are welcomed and anticipated, presenters set the stage for a more engaging and collaborative exchange.

The chapter underscores the importance of active listening during Q&A, urging presenters to attentively understand each question before formulating responses. This not only demonstrates respect for the audience but also contributes to clearer and more relevant answers.

Strategies for Effective Question Handling

A significant portion of Chapter 8 is dedicated to strategies for effective question handling. Presenters are guided through techniques for addressing a variety of questions, from straightforward queries to more challenging or unexpected ones. The importance of maintaining composure, clarity, and authenticity in responses is emphasized, contributing to a positive and professional interaction with the audience.

Readers are prompted to anticipate potential questions, preparing thoughtful responses that align with the presentation's key messages. By approaching questions with a strategic mindset, presenters can enhance the overall coherence and impact of their presentations.

Navigating Challenging Questions

The narrative unfolds into the realm of challenging questions, acknowledging that not all inquiries are straightforward. Presenters are empowered with techniques for navigating challenging or sensitive queries with grace and professionalism. The chapter explores the art of reframing questions, redirecting focus, and acknowledging limitations when necessary.

Strategies for handling questions that may challenge the presenter's credibility or the presentation's core message are discussed. By adopting a proactive and transparent approach, presenters can turn challenging questions into opportunities for clarification and reinforcement of key points.

Encouraging Audience Feedback

Chapter 8 places a spotlight on the significance of audience feedback as a valuable resource for improvement. Presenters are guided through techniques for encouraging constructive feedback, whether through live polls, anonymous surveys, or post-presentation evaluations. By actively seeking and appreciating audience feedback, presenters demonstrate a commitment to continuous improvement and audience satisfaction.

The chapter explores the art of receiving feedback gracefully, emphasizing the importance of maintaining a receptive attitude. Presenters are encouraged to view feedback not as criticism but as valuable insights that contribute to their growth and development as effective communicators.

Implementing Feedback for Improvement

The narrative concludes with a focus on implementing feedback for continuous improvement. Presenters are guided through the process of analysing feedback, identifying patterns, and incorporating constructive suggestions into future presentations. The ability to learn from audience feedback enhances a presenter's adaptability and responsiveness to the evolving needs and expectations of their audience.

In essence, Chapter 8 serves as a guidebook for presenters navigating the interactive phase of presentations. By creating an inclusive Q&A atmosphere, developing strategies for effective question handling, navigating challenging inquiries, encouraging audience feedback, and implementing feedback for improvement, presenters are equipped to transform audience interaction into a collaborative and enriching experience. As the chapter concludes, readers are invited to embrace questions and feedback not as hurdles but as stepping stones toward achieving excellence in their presentation endeavours.

Building Confidence

As the narrative unfolds in Chapter 9, the focus turns to the internal landscape of the presenter the intricate dance of emotions, mindset, and self-assurance that collectively form the foundation of a confident presentation. This chapter explores the multifaceted nature of confidence, offering insights, strategies, and techniques to empower presenters in navigating the psychological aspects of effective communication.

Understanding the Role of Confidence

The chapter commences by delving into the pivotal role of confidence in the presentation journey. Confidence is positioned not as an elusive quality possessed by a select few but as a dynamic and cultivatable attribute that significantly influences audience perception. Readers are prompted to recognize that confidence is not solely about outward expression but also about the presenter's internal mindset and belief in their message.

The importance of authenticity in building confidence is underscored, emphasizing that genuine self-assurance arises from a harmonious alignment between the presenter's beliefs, knowledge, and delivery.

Mindset Shifts for Confidence

A significant portion of the chapter is dedicated to mindset shifts that contribute to building confidence. Presenters are guided through techniques to reframe self-limiting beliefs, quiet the inner critic, and foster a positive and empowering mindset. The chapter explores the psychology of confidence, encouraging presenters to view challenges as opportunities for growth and learning.

The concept of visualization is introduced as a powerful tool for building confidence. By mentally rehearsing successful presentations and envisioning positive outcomes, presenters can cultivate a mindset of success that translates into tangible confidence during actual presentations.

Preparation and Familiarity

The narrative unfolds into the realm of preparation and familiarity as foundational elements of confidence. Presenters are guided through strategies for thorough preparation, emphasizing the importance of knowing the content inside out. The chapter explores techniques for developing a strong familiarity with the presentation space, equipment, and potential challenges, contributing to a sense of control and assurance.

Readers are encouraged to adopt proactive measures, such as rehearsing in the actual presentation venue, testing equipment in advance, and anticipating potential scenarios. By minimizing uncertainties, presenters enhance their confidence and readiness for the presentation.

Effective Stress Management

Chapter 9 places a spotlight on the relationship between stress management and confidence. Presenters are guided through techniques to manage nervous energy and performance anxiety effectively. The chapter explores the power of controlled breathing, mindfulness, and positive affirmations as tools to mitigate stress and enhance a presenter's sense of calm and self-assurance.

Strategies for reframing stress as a natural and adaptive response are discussed, empowering presenters to channel nervous energy into dynamic and engaging presentations.

Embracing Mistakes and Imperfections

As the narrative unfolds, the chapter explores the liberating concept of embracing mistakes and imperfections as allies in the journey to confidence. Presenters are guided to shift their perspective on errors, viewing them not as failures but as opportunities for growth and connection with the audience.

Techniques for gracefully handling unexpected challenges during presentations, such as technical glitches or unforeseen questions, are shared. By adopting a mindset of resilience and adaptability, presenters can navigate uncertainties with confidence and poise.

Post-Presentation Reflection for Growth

The chapter concludes with a focus on post-presentation reflection as a catalyst for ongoing growth in confidence. Presenters are encouraged to engage in constructive self-evaluation, identifying strengths and areas for improvement after each presentation. The ability to extract lessons from experiences contributes to a continuous refinement of skills and an evolving sense of confidence.

In essence, Chapter 9 serves as a comprehensive guide for presenters seeking to cultivate and nurture confidence in their presentation endeavours. By understanding the role of confidence, adopting mindset shifts, prioritizing preparation and familiarity, managing stress effectively, embracing mistakes, and engaging in post-presentation reflection, presenters can build a robust foundation of self-assurance that enhances their impact on the audience. As the chapter concludes, readers are invited to embark on a journey of self-discovery and empowerment, recognizing that confidence is not an endpoint but a dynamic and evolving aspect of their presentation prowess.

Continuous Improvement and Lifelong Learning

As the narrative unfolds in Chapter 10, the spotlight turns to the overarching principle of continuous improvement and lifelong learning an ethos that transcends individual presentations and encapsulates the dynamic journey of evolving as a skilled and impactful communicator. This chapter explores the mindset, strategies, and practices that underpin a commitment to continuous growth, ensuring that presenters remain agile, relevant, and adept in the ever-evolving landscape of effective communication.

The Evolutionary Nature of Presentations

The chapter commences by establishing the evolutionary nature of presentations. In a world characterized by rapid changes in technology, communication trends, and audience expectations, the ability to adapt and evolve is paramount. Readers are prompted to view presentations not as static events but as opportunities for iterative refinement and enhancement.

Understanding that each presentation contributes to an ongoing learning journey, the chapter positions continuous improvement as a mindset that permeates every aspect of a presenter's approach.

Embracing Feedback as a Catalyst for Growth

A significant portion of the chapter is dedicated to the role of feedback as a catalyst for growth. Presenters are guided through the practice of actively seeking feedback from diverse sources, including colleagues, mentors, and audience members. The chapter emphasizes the importance of cultivating a receptive attitude, viewing feedback not as criticism but as valuable insights that contribute to skill refinement.

Readers are encouraged to go beyond formal feedback sessions and proactively seek insights after each presentation. By leveraging feedback as a mirror that reflects strengths and areas for improvement, presenters position themselves for continuous growth.

Setting and Revisiting Personal Development Goals

The narrative unfolds into the realm of goal-setting as a foundational practice for continuous improvement. Presenters are guided through the process of setting clear and specific goals related to their presentation skills. Whether it's enhancing vocal variety, refining visual design, or mastering new technologies, the chapter explores the art of creating goals that are measurable, achievable, and aligned with the presenter's aspirations.

The importance of revisiting and adjusting goals in response to evolving needs and experiences is underscored. Presenters are prompted to view goal-setting not as a static exercise but as a dynamic and responsive practice that aligns with their continuous improvement journey.

Exploring Emerging Technologies and Trends

Chapter 10 places a spotlight on the exploration of emerging technologies and communication trends as a pathway to staying relevant and innovative. Presenters are encouraged to embrace a curious and forward-thinking mindset, actively seeking to integrate new tools and techniques into their presentations.

The chapter explores how technologies such as virtual reality, interactive presentations, or live polling can enhance engagement and elevate the presentation experience. By staying informed about industry trends and technological advancements, presenters position themselves as adaptable and forward-looking communicators.

Commitment to Lifelong Learning

The narrative concludes with a focus on the commitment to lifelong learning as a foundational principle for continuous improvement. Presenters are guided through the value of ongoing education, whether through formal courses, workshops, or self-directed learning. The chapter explores the role of curiosity and a growth mindset in fostering a commitment to continuous learning.

Readers are encouraged to embrace diverse learning modalities, from reading relevant literature to attending conferences and participating in online communities. By maintaining an appetite for learning, presenters not only expand their knowledge base but also infuse their presentations with fresh insights and perspectives.

Cultivating a Growth Mindset

A pivotal theme throughout the chapter is the cultivation of a growth mindset an outlook that embraces challenges, persists in the face of setbacks, and sees effort as a path to mastery. Presenters are guided to view each presentation, whether successful or challenging, as a stepping stone toward growth and improvement.

Strategies for overcoming setbacks, reframing failures as opportunities, and celebrating progress are explored. By cultivating a growth mindset, presenters create a resilient foundation that propels them forward in their continuous improvement journey.

In essence, Chapter 10 serves as a manifesto for presenters committed to the principles of continuous improvement and lifelong learning. By embracing feedback, setting and revisiting personal development goals, exploring emerging technologies, and cultivating a growth mindset, presenters can navigate the dynamic landscape of effective communication with agility and relevance. As the chapter concludes, readers are invited to view their presentation journey not as a finite series of events but as an ongoing odyssey of growth, adaptation, and mastery.

Navigating Virtual Presentations

In the unfolding narrative of Chapter 11, the spotlight shifts to the contemporary landscape of virtual presentations—a realm shaped by technology, remote communication, and the evolving dynamics of a digital audience. This chapter serves as a comprehensive guide, offering insights, strategies, and best practices for presenters navigating the unique challenges and opportunities presented by virtual platforms.

Understanding the Virtual Presentation Landscape

The chapter commences by providing a nuanced understanding of the virtual presentation landscape. Presenters are guided through the distinctive characteristics of virtual communication, acknowledging factors such as screen fatigue, varying technological proficiency, and the absence of physical presence. Readers are prompted to recognize that effective virtual presentations require tailored approaches that transcend traditional in-person methodologies.

Leveraging Technology for Engagement

A significant portion of the chapter is dedicated to the strategic use of technology to enhance engagement in virtual presentations. Presenters are guided through the selection and mastery of virtual tools and platforms, emphasizing considerations such as ease of use, accessibility, and interactive features. The chapter explores how technologies like video conferencing, collaborative documents, and virtual whiteboards can be harnessed to foster engagement and participation.

Strategies for navigating potential technical challenges, from audio issues to screen sharing intricacies, are discussed. By becoming adept at leveraging technology, presenters can create seamless and engaging virtual experiences for their audience.

Adapting Presentation Styles for Virtual Platforms

The narrative unfolds into the realm of adapting presentation styles to suit the nuances of virtual platforms. Presenters are encouraged to consider factors such as camera presence, lighting, and background aesthetics. The chapter explores techniques for maintaining eye contact through the camera, optimizing lighting for visibility, and creating a professional and uncluttered virtual background.

The importance of vocal modulation and clear articulation is underscored in the context of virtual presentations. Presenters are guided through the nuances of pacing, tone, and emphasis that contribute to audience engagement in a digital setting.

Fostering Interaction and Participation

Chapter 11 places a spotlight on the imperative of fostering interaction and participation in virtual presentations. Strategies for overcoming the potential disconnect of virtual platforms and creating a sense of connection with the audience are explored. The chapter introduces techniques such as interactive polls, virtual breakout sessions, and Q&A segments to keep the audience engaged and actively participating.

Presenters are encouraged to embrace the chat feature as a tool for real-time interaction, allowing for questions, comments, and engagement throughout the presentation. By fostering a dynamic and interactive virtual environment, presenters can transcend the limitations of physical distance and captivate their digital audience.

Ensuring Accessibility and Inclusivity

The chapter unfolds into the principle of ensuring accessibility and inclusivity in virtual presentations. Presenters are guided through practices that accommodate diverse audience needs, from providing closed captions to choosing fonts and colors that enhance readability. The chapter explores the importance of clear navigation and instructions for virtual platforms, ensuring that all participants can seamlessly navigate the presentation.

Strategies for accommodating different time zones and scheduling considerations are discussed, recognizing the global nature of virtual audiences. By prioritizing accessibility, presenters contribute to an inclusive and equitable virtual experience for all participants.

Navigating Challenges and Unexpected Interruptions

A pivotal theme throughout Chapter 11 is the proactive navigation of challenges and unexpected interruptions in the virtual realm. Presenters are guided through techniques for handling disruptions, whether they stem from technical issues, background noise, or unexpected interruptions. The chapter explores the importance of maintaining composure, adaptability, and a sense of humour in the face of unforeseen challenges.

Strategies for pre-emptively addressing potential technical issues, such as testing equipment in advance and having contingency plans, are shared. By approaching virtual presentations with a prepared and resilient mindset, presenters can navigate challenges with grace and professionalism.

Conclusion: Mastering the Art of Virtual Presentation

In conclusion, Chapter 11 serves as a guidebook for presenters navigating the complex and dynamic terrain of virtual presentations. By understanding the virtual landscape, leveraging technology for engagement, adapting presentation styles, fostering interaction, ensuring accessibility, and navigating challenges, presenters can master the art of virtual communication. As the chapter concludes, readers are invited to embrace the opportunities presented by virtual platforms and to continuously refine their skills to meet the evolving expectations of the digital audience.

Cultivating Authenticity in Presentations

In the unfolding narrative of Chapter 12, the spotlight turns to the timeless and transformative quality of authenticity—an essential element that transcends presentation techniques and methodologies, connecting presenters with their audience on a deep and meaningful level. This chapter explores the essence of authenticity, offering insights, strategies, and practices to help presenters cultivate a genuine and compelling presence in their communication endeavours.

The Power of Authenticity

The chapter commences by delving into the intrinsic power of authenticity in presentations. Presenters are guided to recognize authenticity not as a mere performance strategy but as a fundamental aspect of human connection. Authenticity establishes a bridge between the presenter and the audience, fostering trust, relatability, and resonance.

Understanding that authenticity extends beyond words to encompass body language, tone, and intent, the chapter positions it as a cornerstone that underpins every aspect of effective communication.

Aligning Values and Messaging

A significant portion of the chapter is dedicated to the alignment of values and messaging as a pathway to authenticity. Presenters are guided through the process of identifying and embracing their core values, ensuring that these values permeate their messaging. The chapter explores how authenticity arises when the presenter's beliefs and intentions align seamlessly with the content being delivered.

Readers are prompted to reflect on the congruence between their personal values and the messages they convey in presentations. By fostering this alignment, presenters not only enhance their authenticity but also create presentations that resonate with sincerity.

Connecting with Personal Stories

The narrative unfolds into the realm of personal stories as catalysts for authenticity. Presenters are encouraged to share relevant anecdotes, experiences, and narratives that provide a glimpse into their personal journey. The chapter explores how personal stories create a humanizing effect, allowing the audience to connect with the presenter on a deeper level.

Strategies for crafting and integrating personal stories into presentations are discussed. By sharing authentic narratives, presenters add layers of relatability and emotion to their message, elevating the overall impact on the audience.

Embracing Vulnerability

Chapter 12 places a spotlight on the concept of embracing vulnerability as a courageous act of authenticity. Presenters are guided to recognize that vulnerability is not a sign of weakness but a testament to transparency and genuine connection. The chapter explores how moments of vulnerability, whether acknowledging challenges or expressing genuine emotions, can resonate profoundly with the audience.

Strategies for navigating vulnerability with authenticity are shared. Presenters are encouraged to embrace their authentic selves, even in moments of uncertainty, inviting the audience into a shared space of openness and authenticity.

Authentic Body Language and Vocal Expression

The chapter unfolds into the exploration of authentic body language and vocal expression. Presenters are guided through techniques to align their non-verbal cues with their authentic message. The importance of natural gestures, facial expressions, and vocal modulation is underscored in conveying sincerity and genuine engagement.

Readers are prompted to observe and enhance their own body language and vocal expression, ensuring that these elements harmonize with the authenticity of their message. By cultivating a congruent and authentic physical presence, presenters strengthen their overall impact.

Navigating the Balance: Professionalism vs. Authenticity

A pivotal theme throughout Chapter 12 is the delicate balance between professionalism and authenticity. Presenters are guided through strategies for maintaining professionalism while embracing authenticity. The chapter explores how authenticity can coexist with preparedness, ensuring that spontaneity and genuine connection do not compromise the overall structure and professionalism of the presentation.

Strategies for infusing authenticity into various presentation formats, from formal business presentations to more casual settings, are discussed. By navigating this balance thoughtfully, presenters create an authentic yet polished presentation style.

Cultivating Authenticity Through Preparation and Practice

The chapter concludes with a focus on cultivating authenticity through preparation and practice. Presenters are guided to view preparation not as a hindrance to authenticity but as a facilitator. The chapter explores how thorough preparation provides a solid foundation, allowing presenters to speak from a place of confidence and authenticity.

The importance of practice, not to memorize a script but to internalize the key messages and enhance comfort with the content, is emphasized. By embracing preparation and practice as allies, presenters can navigate the presentation space with authenticity and poise.

In essence, Chapter 12 serves as a guide for presenters seeking to cultivate authenticity in their communication. By understanding the power of authenticity, aligning values with messaging, connecting through personal stories, embracing vulnerability, incorporating authentic body language and vocal expression, navigating the balance between professionalism and authenticity, and cultivating authenticity through preparation and practice, presenters can elevate their communication to a level that resonates deeply with their audience. As the chapter concludes, readers are invited to embrace authenticity not as a strategy but as a profound and transformative approach to meaningful and impactful presentations.

The Culmination: Mastering the Art of Impactful Presentations

As we arrive at the culmination of this journey through the art and science of impactful presentations, Chapter 13 serves as the concluding chapter—a reflective and integrative exploration that encapsulates the key principles, strategies, and insights gathered throughout the preceding chapters. This chapter serves as a guidepost for presenters on the path to mastery, providing a holistic perspective on the multifaceted journey of effective communication.

Reflecting on the Presentation Journey

The chapter begins with a moment of reflection, inviting presenters to revisit the evolution of their presentation journey. From the foundational principles of effective communication to the nuances of virtual presentations and the cultivation of authenticity, this chapter prompts readers to reflect on their growth, challenges, and triumphs. It acknowledges that the journey to mastery is an ongoing process, marked by continuous learning and adaptation.

The Four Pillars of Impactful Presentations

Chapter 13 introduces the concept of the Four Pillars of Impactful Presentations, drawing from the diverse themes explored in the preceding chapters:

Content Mastery: The foundation of impactful presentations lies in a deep and nuanced understanding of the content. Presenters are encouraged to approach content creation with clarity, relevance, and a keen awareness of the audience's needs.

Engaging Delivery: The art of engaging delivery transforms information into a dynamic and memorable experience. This pillar emphasizes the importance of vocal variety, pacing, interactive techniques, and adaptability to captivate and connect with the audience.

Audience Interaction and Adaptability: Recognizing the dynamic interplay between presenters and their audience, this pillar underscores the significance of fostering interaction, navigating questions and feedback, and adapting to diverse audience needs and preferences.

Authenticity and Continuous Improvement: The final pillar encapsulates the essence of authenticity and the commitment to continuous improvement. Authenticity, rooted in personal values, transparency, and genuine connection, is positioned as the cornerstone of impactful presentations. The commitment to lifelong learning and growth serves as the catalyst for mastery.

Cultivating a Personalized Presentation Style

Building on the Four Pillars, Chapter 13 guides presenters in cultivating a personalized presentation style that aligns with their unique strengths, personality, and communication goals. It encourages presenters to embrace their authenticity, allowing it to shine through in their content, delivery, and interactions. The chapter recognizes that while principles and techniques are valuable guides, each presenter possesses a distinctive style that can elevate their impact.

The Ever-Evolving Landscape of Presentations

Acknowledging the ever-evolving landscape of presentations, the chapter explores the impact of emerging technologies, virtual platforms, and changing audience expectations. Presenters are urged to stay abreast of technological advancements, trends, and best practices, adapting their approach to meet the evolving needs of their audience.

Embracing Challenges as Opportunities for Growth

Chapter 13 reframes challenges as opportunities for growth and refinement. Whether navigating technical issues in virtual presentations, handling tough questions, or embracing vulnerability, the chapter encourages presenters to view challenges not as roadblocks but as stepping stones toward mastery. It emphasizes the resilience and adaptability required to thrive in the dynamic and sometimes unpredictable world of presentations.

The Journey Continues: Lifelong Learning and Mastery

In the final pages, Chapter 13 serves as a reminder that the journey to mastery is a lifelong pursuit. Lifelong learning, continuous reflection, and a commitment to growth are positioned as the hallmarks of a masterful presenter. The chapter concludes with an invitation for presenters to embark on their continued journey, armed with the insights, skills, and authenticity cultivated throughout this exploration of impactful presentations.

As the book draws to a close, readers are reminded that mastery is not a destination but a dynamic and ever-unfolding process. The principles and strategies shared throughout the chapters serve as enduring companions on the path to becoming a skilled, impactful, and authentic communicator. The concluding chapter resonates as both a culmination and a commencement—a celebration of the progress made and an invitation to embrace the ongoing evolution of mastering the art of impactful presentations.